Olympic Gold

Scott Frothingham

Olympic Gold

Other books by Scott Frothingham:

Olympic Gold #2
Olympic Spirit
Mount Rushmore Motivation
6-Minute Success Training
Success-ercize

Published by
FastForwardPublishing.com

Copyright © 2014 by FastForwardPublishing
All rights reserved.

Permission to reproduce or transmit in any form or by any means, electronic or mechanical, including photocopying and recording, or by any information storage or retrieval system, must be obtained in writing from FastForwardPublishing.

This book has been fully researched for factual accuracy. The authors and publishers cannot assume responsibility for any errors or omissions. The reader assumes all responsibilities for any loss or damages, whether consequential, incidental or otherwise that may result from the information presented in this publication.

We rely on our experience and thorough research processes to determine that the information presented in this book is as factual and well thought out as possible. In the event that any material is incorrect or not appropriately attributed, please contact us and we will make any necessary changes or additions, as quickly as possible.

Please feel free to share this book with family and friends. If you feel others may benefit from this book, you can make them aware of how to access the book so they can download a copy if they so choose.

Images are from Royalty Free (licensed) image repositories and from photographic sites, through Creative Commons, and include the necessary attributions.

Photo Credits page 89

ISBN-10: 1479247774
ISBN-13: 9781479247776

THANK YOU

To say, "Thanks" for buying this book, we'd like you to have

Go to this web address:
www.FastForwardPublishing.com/Thank-You-Olympic-Gold.html
to get your free copy.

DEDICATION

To my uncle -- Allan S. Woods -- who championed the sport of Men's Field Hockey and served for many years on US Olympic Committee; and to all Olympians – past, present and future – who inspire and motivate us with their drive, discipline, dedication and, ultimately, their performance in the world's largest and most celebrated exhibition of athletic skill and competitive spirit.

CONTENTS

1	Introduction	page	6
2	Behind the Competition	page	7
3	Olympic Gold Quotes	page	9
4	Olympic Gold #2	page	81
5	About the Author	page	82
6	A Request	page	83
5	Featured Quote Details	page	85
7	Photo Credits	page	89

INTRODUCTION

"For too long the world has failed to recognize that the Olympic Games and the Olympic Movement are about fine athletics and fine art." -Avery Brundage

The Olympic Games serve as a peace sign for the people of the world to come together and bond for a single purpose.

> *"The Olympic Games are the quadrennial celebration of the springtime of humanity."* -Pierre de Coubertin

It is a showcase of the human competitive spirit, representing the good of sport that often goes overlooked in today's world ... a showcase of athletic glory, a test of what the most raw of talent can do against the rest of humanity's best.

> *"Most other competitions are individual achievements, but the Olympic Games is something that belongs to everybody."* -Scott Hamilton

There are lessons to be learned from this awe-inspiring struggle of sport that gives us the opportunity to think of all the blood, sweat and tears these athletes have devoted to get to the Games and of the countless others who have given all the same but who did not.

I hope you enjoy this selection of over 140 inspiring, motivating and insightful quotes from those dedicated athletes whose performance rose above the rest to bring them to Olympic victory.

R. Scott Frothingham
www.FastForwardincome.com
A Resource for Entrepreneurs,
Managers and Sales Professionals

BEHIND THE COMPETITION

The Olympic Motto

In 1921, Pierre de Coubertin, founder of the modern Olympic Games, borrowed a Latin phrase from his friend, Father Henri Didon, for the Olympic motto: Citius, Altius, Fortius which translates to "Swifter, Higher, Stronger".

The Olympic Oath

Pierre de Coubertin wrote an oath for the athletes to recite at each Olympic Games: "In the name of all competitors, I promise that we shall take part in these Olympic Games, respecting and abiding by the rules that govern them, in the true spirit of sportsmanship, for the glory of sport and the honor of our teams." During the opening ceremonies, one athlete recites the oath on behalf of all the athletes.

The Olympic Creed

The Olympic Creed reads: "The most important thing in the Olympic Games is not to win but to take part, just as the most important thing in life is not the triumph but the struggle. The essential thing is not to have conquered but to have fought well." Pierre de Coubertin was inspired by a speech given by Bishop Ethelbert Talbot at a service for Olympic champions during the 1908 Olympic Games.

The Official Olympic Flag

Created by Pierre de Coubertin in 1914, the Olympic flag contains five interconnected rings on a white background. The five rings symbolize the five significant continents and are interconnected to symbolize the friendship to be gained from these international competitions. The rings, from left to right, are blue, yellow, black, green, and red. The colors were chosen because at least one of them appeared on the flag of every country in the world. The Olympic flag was first flown during the 1920 Olympic Games.

OLYMPIC GOLD:
140+ Inspirational, Motivational
& Insightful Quotes
featuring Olympic Medal Winners

"I have been visualizing myself every night for the past four years standing on the podium having the gold placed around my neck." - Megan Quann, 3 time Olympic medalist - swimming

"If you can pick up after a crushing defeat, and go on to win again, you are going to be a champion someday." -Wilma Rudolph, 3 time Olympic medalist - track and field

"If you're trying to achieve, there will be roadblocks. I've had them; everybody has had them. But obstacles don't have to stop you. If you run into a wall, don't turn around and give up. Figure out how to climb it, go through it, or work around it." -Michael Jordan, 2 time Olympic medalist - basketball

"And then ultimately what I tell the kids is: coaches can give you information, they can give you guidelines, and they can put you in a position. But the only person who can truly make you better is you." -Brandi Chastain, 3 time Olympic medalist - Football/Soccer

Scott Frothingham

> "A champion is afraid of losing. Everyone else is afraid of winning."
>
> Billie Jean King

Olympic Gold

"I am a big believer in visualization. I run through my races mentally so that I feel even more prepared." -Allyson Felix, 6 time Olympic medalist - track and field

OPENING CEREMONY
2008 Olympic Games - Olympic Opening Ceremony
'One World, One Dream'

"I hated every minute of training, but I said, 'Don't quit. Suffer now and live the rest of your life as a champion'." -Muhammad Ali, 1 time Olympic medalist - boxing

"The water is your friend.....you don't have to fight with water, just share the same spirit as the water, and it will help you move." - Alexandr Popov, 9 time Olympic medalist - swimming

Scott Frothingham

"Adversity, if you allow it to, will fortify you and make you the best you can be."

Kerri Walsh Jennings

"The U.S. Olympic spirit award is an award that is given to an athlete who embodies the Olympic spirit in more ways than just on the playing field, in showing incredible perseverance, in overcoming obstacles ..." -Brian Boitano, 1 time Olympic medalist - figure skating

"'Breathe, believe, and battle.' My former coach, Troy Tanner, told us that before each match. Breathe-be in the moment. Believe-have faith that you can rise above it. Battle-you gotta be prepared to go for as long as it takes." -Kerri Walsh, 3 time Olympic gold medalist - beach volleyball

"The medals don't mean anything and the glory doesn't last. It's all about your happiness. The rewards are going to come, but my happiness is just loving the sport and having fun performing." - Jackie Joyner-Kersee, 6 time Olympic medalist - track and field

"I run to be known as the greatest runner, the greatest of all time. I could not eat or sleep for a week after I lost in the (1992) Olympics. I have to win or die." -Noureddine Morceli, 1 time Olympic medalist - track and field

"I believe that you should gravitate to people who are doing productive and positive things with their lives." -Nadia Comaneci, 9 time Olympic medalist - gymnastics

Scott Frothingham

"Ask yourself: 'Can I give more?'. The answer is usually: 'Yes'."

Paul Tergat

Olympic Gold

OLYMPIC TORCH
2012 Olympics Games

Scott Frothingham

"Don't put a limit on anything. The more you dream, the further you get."

Michael Phelps

"My thoughts before a big race are usually pretty simple. I tell myself: 'Get out of the blocks, run your race, stay relaxed. If you run your race, you'll win... channel your energy. Focus.'" -Carl Lewis, 10 time Olympic medalist - track and field

"I was introverted, shy. But if you win a lot you need to be extroverted, or they'll think you're arrogant." -Alberto Tomba, 5 time Olympic medalist - skiing

"I don't like to look at it as competition. It's about me conquering myself... me being able to face my own fears, distractions, and weaknesses and say that I overcame them." -Apolo Ohno, 8 time Olympic medalist - short track speed skating

"I saw my name: THOMAS, Petria. Saw my time, 57.72. Saw the number one next to them. I'd done it. Me! Petria Thomas, Olympic champion. The feeling inside was one of pure, utter joy. Excitement, disbelief, relief, happiness, amazement, the whole works. I'd worked so hard. I'd gone through so much, privately, publicly. I'd lost faith in myself and found it again. I'd sometimes stopped believing that I could do it and that I had a purpose in life. I'd come through the darkness, and this, this moment, was the sweetest, most amazing light there could possibly be. I was alive and loving it!" -Petria Thomas, 8 time Olympic medalist - swimming

"A lifetime of training for just ten seconds." - Jesse Owens, 4 time Olympic medalist - track and field

> "Each of us has a fire in our hearts for something. It's our goal in life to find it and keep it lit."
>
> Mary Lou Retton

BASKETBALL
2008 Olympic Games - Men's Basketball - USA vs. China

"He who is not courageous enough to take risks will accomplish nothing in life."

Muhammad Ali

"Something my mom taught me when I was little is that everything happens for a reason. Retiring was scary and it was tough to give up gymnastics, but so many great opportunities have come from it that I never expected. And those wouldn't have happened had I not accepted my injury as a way to try something new." -Shawn Johnson, 4 time Olympic medalist - gymnastics

"Every time I fail, I assume I will be a stronger person for it. I keep on running figuratively and literally, despite a limp that gets more noticeable with each passing season, because for me there has always been a place to go and a terrible urgency to get there." -Joan Benoit Samuelson, 1 time Olympic medalist - track and field

"There is something in the Olympics, indefinable, springing from the soul, that must be preserved." -Chris Brasher, 1 time Olympic medalist - track and field

"We make choices. I hate to say 'sacrifices.' When I speak to younger groups, to colleges and other younger athletes, I say 'we don't make sacrifices. If we truly love this sport and we have these goals and dreams in the sport, the classroom, or in life, they're not sacrifices. They're choices that we make to fulfill these goals and dreams.' Sacrifices makes it sound like 'oh, poor me, I have to do this in order to get to this,' and I don't really like that word. It was just really the choice to take care of myself and live a proper lifestyle. In doing that, I feel like a healthier person, I feel focused in everything, not just in my running. In following this one dream, I feel like I became an even more well-rounded person." -Deena Kastor, 1 time Olympic medalist, track and field

Scott Frothingham

"I didn't set out to beat the world; I just set out to do my absolute best."

Al Oerter

Olympic Gold

EQUESTRIAN
2008 Olympic Games - Equestrian game day ceremony in Sha Tin

"Spend at least some of your training time, and other parts of your day, concentrating on what you are doing in training and visualizing your success." -Grete Waitz, 1 time Olympic medalist, track and field

"Perhaps I don't give the impression that I'm hurting on the track. But that is because I am animated by an interior force which covers my suffering." -Noureddine Morceli, 1 time Olympic medalist - track and field

"It has been said that the Opening Ceremony of the Olympic Games is something that an athlete will remember for the rest of their life. It is true. That moment when you walk into the Olympic Stadium as part of the Australian Olympic Team, is a moment that I will never forget."- Jeff Fenech, 1 Olympic games - boxing

"I concentrate on preparing to swim my race and let the other swimmers think about me, not me about them." -Amanda Beard, 7 time Olympic medalist - swimming

"Nothing can substitute for just plain hard work. I had to put in the time to get back. And it was a grind. It meant training and sweating every day. But I was completely committed to working out to prove to myself that I still could do it." -Andre Agassi, 1 time Olympic medalist - tennis

Scott Frothingham

> "I made a mistake but I came back to show the world that I'm still the best."
>
> Usain Bolt

Olympic Gold

GYMNASTICS
2008 Olympic Games - Trampoline

"I set my sights on making an Olympic team, not realizing how tough it was going to be."

Jackie Joyner-Kersee

"I can't see myself leaving the club I grew up supporting... it's one of those things, the money's great but I still get paid reasonably well from the Lions and at the end of the day I think job satisfaction is the No.1 priority and I just love it up here." -Jonathan Brown, 1 Olympic games - track and field

"As a sportsman, I accept being beaten. Everybody tries to be a winner, but only one in a race will win. It's fun to win. But I don't find unhappiness if I lose." -Kip Keino, 4 time Olympic medalist - track and field

"I tell people I'm too stupid to know what's impossible. I have ridiculously large dreams, and half the time they come true." -Debi Thomas, 1 time Olympic medalist - figure skating

"If one can stick to the training throughout the many long years, then will power is no longer a problem. It's raining? That doesn't matter. I am tired? That's besides the point. It's simply that I just have to." - Emil Zatopek, 5 time Olympic medalist - track and field

"The Athens Olympics will be meaningful even though I cannot participate as an athlete, since I can participate in the flame relay all over the world." -Cathy Freeman, 2 time Olympic medalist - track and field

"I think the way to become the best is to just have fun."

Shaun White

Olympic Gold

"When runners win a big race these days, they get a car. When I won a big race, I got a ride." -Ron Delany, 1 time Olympic medalist - track and field

TRACK & FIELD
2000 Olympic Games - Women's Long Jump

"The most important thing in the Olympic Games is not winning, but taking part; the essential thing in life is not conquering but fighting well." - Pierre de Coubertin, founder of modern Olympic Games.

Scott Frothingham

"If you think you're done, you always have at least 40% more."

Lauren Crandall

"I'm not used to crying. It's a little difficult. All my life I've had to fight. It's just another fight I'm going to have to learn how to win, that's all. I'm just going to have to keep smiling." -Serena Williams, 4 time Olympic medalist - tennis

"'Keep calm and carry on.' A challenging time is just that-a period in time. Taking a few deep breaths and knowing that it won't last forever really allows me to focus on the present moment and task at hand." -Betsey Armstrong, 2 time Olympic medalist - water polo

"Never underestimate the power of dreams and the influence of the human spirit. We are all the same in this notion: The potential for greatest lives within each of us." -Wilma Rudolph, 3 time Olympic medalist - track and field

"I try and just relax and reflect on all the work I've done in the past season. That's one of the most important things, remembering your goals and how to swim your races. It's also important to get your mind off racing before you race sometimes." -Ian Crocker, 5 time Olympic medalist - swimming

"It took me time to realize that the men who won Olympic gold medals in the decathlon are just men, just like me." -Dan O'Brien, 3 time Olympic medalist - track and field

Scott Frothingham

> "You never know what can happen. I feel like I have a pretty good chance, but you never know."
>
> Carly Patterson

Olympic Gold

> "If you win through bad sportsmanship, that's no real victory."
>
> Babe Didrikson Zaharias

"Do I feel any pressure as the most decorated Winter Olympian in American history? None at all. The only pressures that I know I face are those of how to pay it forward: How can I continually make a positive impact in people's lives, help others achieve their dreams, create their own Olympic mindset, creating champions within themselves?" -Apolo Ohno, 8 time Olympic medalist - short track speed skating

CYCLING
Olympic Games 2012 - Men's Road Race - Headley Heath, on the Box Hill circuit.

"Being in school is the best place to be if you are an athlete because you can structure your own time." -Frank Shorter, 2 time Olympic medalist - track and field

> "Ingenuity plus courage plus work equals miracles."
>
> Bob Richards

WEIGHTLIFTING
2012 Olympic Games - Women's 75kg

"I can definitely take more off my world record - a lot more. I have no doubt about that. I'm by no means putting pressure on myself, it's just the belief I have in myself......I'm not going to limit myself by nominating times or anything like that. I never thought I'd do 14:34 and I did. I thought I'd maybe do 14:38 or 14:39 that day, and I went nearly five seconds quicker so I don't want to limit the possibilities." -Grant Hackett, 7 time Olympic medalist - swimming

> "It is better to look ahead and prepare than to look back and regret."
>
> Jackie Joyner-Kersee

"As an Olympic champion gymnast, I have always stayed involved in my sport." -Nadia Comaneci, 2 time Olympic medalist - gymnastics

"I'm not going to limit myself by nominating times or anything like that. I never thought I'd do 14:34 and I did. I thought I'd maybe do 14:38 or 14:39 that day, and I went nearly five seconds quicker so I don't want to limit the possibilities." -Grant Hackett, 7 time Olympic medalist - swimming

"I've just been enjoying the training a bit more. I've put too much pressure on myself in the past. Just relax and let it come. I just went out there to have a bit of fun tonight." -Sophie Edington, 1 Olympic games - swimming

"I was so surprised. Then again, I was so relaxed in the water, it felt amazing." -Pieter van den Hoogenband, 7 time Olympic medalist - swimming

"When we stage the Olympics it will inspire kids all over the country. A kid in Scotland or Ireland will be encouraged to take up sport." -Daley Thompson, 2 time Olympic medalist - track and field

"Make yourself an example, achieve it, but don't hurt anyone on the way up. I don't think I did that." -Dawn Fraser, 8 time Olympic medalist - swimming

> "It's always an honor to be able to represent your country at the highest level."
>
> Basheer Abdullah

SPECTATORS
Olympic Games 2010 - Men's Hockey – Canada vs. Switzerland

"The greatest memory for me of the 1984 Olympics was not the individual honors, but standing on the podium with my teammates to receive our team gold medal." -Mitch Gaylord, 4 time Olympic medalist - gymnastics

"Acting is easier than skating in a way and harder in other aspects. In skating, you get one chance, and with acting you get to do it over and over." -Tara Lipinski, figure skater - 1 time Olympic medalist

> "It's all about the journey, not the outcome."
>
> Carl Lewis

> "You have to expect things of yourself before you can do them."
>
> Michael Jordan

Olympic Gold

SKIING
2010 Olympic Games - Men's Downhill

"My biggest weakness as a endurance athlete has been in not drinking enough water after training, thereby racing sometimes while dehydrated." -Bill Rodgers, 1 Olympic games - track and field

"I always thought, it would be neat to make the Olympic team." - Michael Phelps, 22 time Olympic medalist - swimming

"Run so hard you come in with bloody feet and missing toenails."

Rob De Castella

"Body does what mind prefers."

Lenny Krayzelburg

"Part of being a champ is acting like a champ. You have to learn how to win and not run away when you lose." -Nancy Kerrigan, 2 time Olympic medalist - figure skating

"Mainly, I like to have fun. Swimming is all about having fun, and I am firm believer that you should keep swimming as long as you are having fun, but I can say that it becomes much more fun as you get older and learn more about the sport, life, and especially more about yourself." -Scott Goldblatt, 2 time Olympic medalist - swimming

"What I can tell them is the way you become an Olympic champion is to start working now. I tell them why it's always worth it to put the time and effort into something you want to be good at." -Rafer Johnson, 2 time Olympic medalist - track and field

"There is the truth about the marathon and very few of you have written the truth. Even if I explain to you, you'll never understand it, you're outside of it." -Douglas Wakiihuri, 1 time Olympic medalist - track and field

"'If you're not having fun, then what the hell are you doing?' It reminds me to find the reason why I'm doing it and why I'm out there, which makes things more manageable when I'm stressed and fatigued." -Allison Jones, Allison Paralympic medals - skiing, cycling

"Steady, ready, poised, winning."

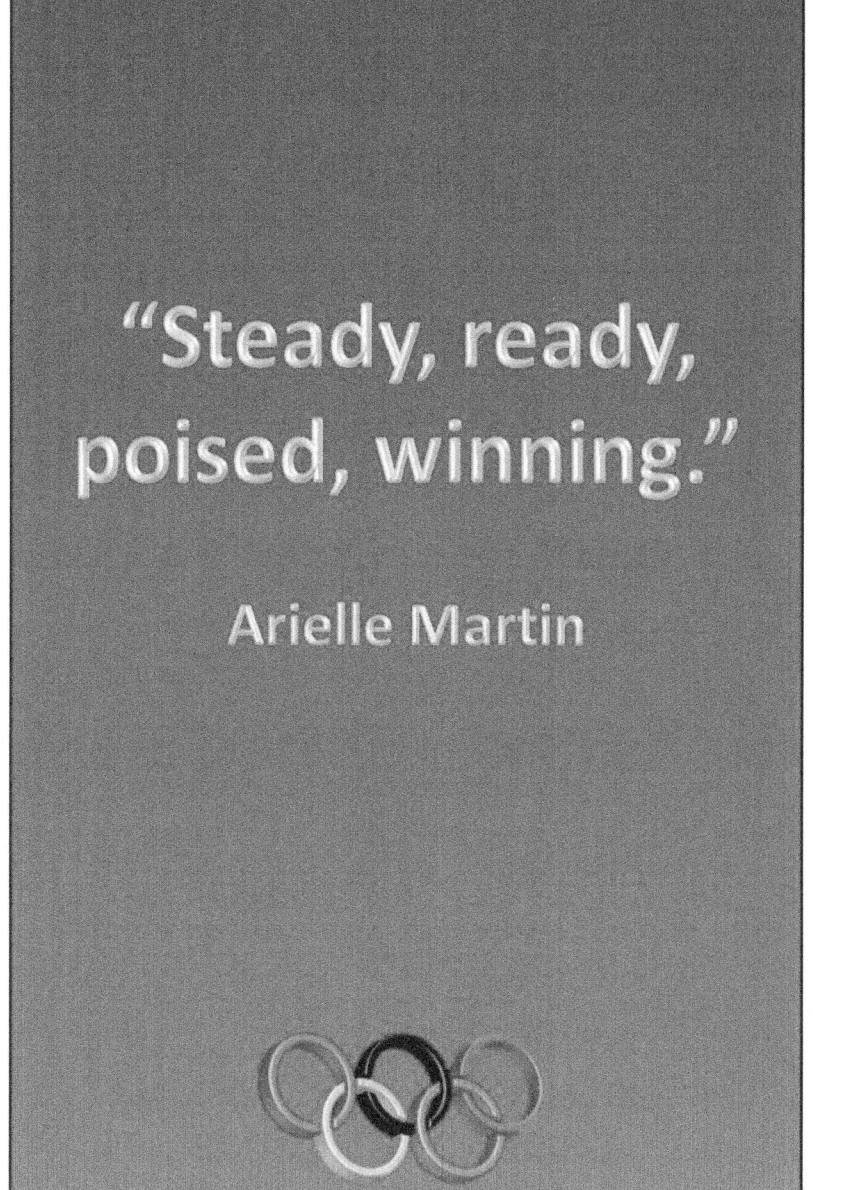

Arielle Martin

Scott Frothingham

"I enjoyed every bit of my swimming career. I think that's the most important advice- to enjoy what you do." -Summer Sanders, 4 time Olympic medalist - swimming

"You always need younger guys if you're going to be successful in the long term." -Saku Koivu, 4 time Olympic medalist - ice hockey

TRACK & FIELD
2012 Olympics Games – Pole Vault

> "Success for an athlete follows many years of hard work and dedication."
>
> Michael Diamond

Scott Frothingham

> "It's not the destination, it's the journey."
>
> Missy Franklin

"Everything that I've ever been able to accomplish in skating and in life has come out of adversity and perseverance." -Scott Hamilton, 1 time Olympic medalist - figure skater

"You have to do something in your life that is honorable and not cowardly if you are to live in peace with yourself." - Larry Brown, head coach Olympic men's basketball

"It really means a lot that I won the gold medal - but I woke up the next morning expecting to feel different. I felt the same." -Dan O'Brien, 3 time Olympic medalist - track and field

"Luck has nothing to do with it, because I have spent many, many hours, countless hours, on the court working for my one moment in time, not knowing when it would come." -Serena Williams, 4 time Olympic medalist - tennis

"I touched the wall and all my dreams, hopes and ambitions basically coalesced into one moment." -Duncan Armstrong, 4 time Olympic medalist - swimming

"I'd rather get a nice warm-up suit. That's something I can use. Gold medals just sit there. When I get old, maybe I could sell them if I need the money." -Eric Heiden, 5 time Olympic medalist - speed skating

Scott Frothingham

> "Surpassing my achievements feels incredible; I want to replicate that again and again."
>
> Katherine Reutter

"My will to live completely overcame my desire to win" - Alfred Hajos, 2 time Olympic medalist - swimming

"I am still young. I have a lot of time. And if someone breaks my records in the future, I won't cry. That's sport." -Noureddine Morceli, 1 time Olympic medalist - track and field

"Scientists have proven that it's impossible to long-jump 30 feet, but I don't listen to that kind of talk. Thoughts like that have a way of sinking into your feet." -Carl Lewis, 10 time Olympic medalist - track and field

"At my age, you need to verify that everything is fine. I put a lot of pressure on my body, and I feel sometimes pain in my back and in my knees, so I have to be sure that I can keep on training hard before going on." -Hermann Maier, 4 time Olympic medalist - skiing

"One word: 'Fight.' Anyone can do it when it feels good. When you're hurting, that's when it makes a difference, so you have to keep fighting." -Erin Cafaro, 2 time Olympic medalist - rowing

"I am stronger than ever." -Jessica Hardy, 2 time Olympic medalist - swimming

> "The difference between the impossible and the possible lies in a person's determination."
>
> Tommy Lasorda

CURLING
2010 Olympic Games

"Olympians are the product of the Movement, and to get them to the stadiums, pools and playing fields, it takes the actions of legions of people who might not be Olympians." -Bill Toomey, 1 time Olympic medalist - track and field

"Nobody needs to prove to anybody what they're worthy of, just the person that they look at in the mirror. That's the only person you need to answer to." -Picabo Street, 2 time Olympic medalist - skiing

> "The first thing is to love your sport. Never do it to please someone else. It has to be yours."
>
> Peggy Fleming

"You have to train your mind like you train your body."

Bruce Jenner

"I think sports gave me the first place where this awkward girl could feel comfortable in my own skin. I think that's true for a lot of women-sports gives you a part of your life where you can work at something and you look in the mirror and you like that person." - Teri McKeever, head coach Olympic women's swimming

"All I've done is run fast. I don't see why people should make much fuss about that." -Fanny Blankers-Koen, 3 time gold medalist - track and field

"Keep your dreams alive. Understand to achieve anything requires faith and belief in yourself, vision, hard work, determination, and dedication. Remember all things are possible for those who believe." -Gail Devers, 3 time Olympic medalist - track and field

"I still can't believe I won the Olympics. That's what I feel right now - completely alive as a human being. It's a really beautiful moment. " - Clara Hughes, 3 time Olympic medalist - cycling and speed skating

"As a teenager I had no idea that I had the potential to win an Olympic gold medal and my athletic career developed only by lucky circumstances." -Peter Snell, 3 time Olympic medalist - track and field

> "You have to have your wits about you and think quickly on your feet."
>
> Michael East

"Somewhere behind the athlete you've become and the hours of practice and the coaches who have pushed you is a little girl who fell in love with the game and never looked back... play for her." -Mia Hamm, 3 Time Olympic Medalist - soccer/football

SWIMMING
2012 Olympics Games – Men's Butterfly

"What was most important to me at the Olympics was going out there and performing my best. When I messed up the first jump combination, which was my big move, it hit me that I messed up the program of my life." -Debi Thomas, 1 time Olympic medalist - figure skating

Olympic Gold

> "There's no such thing as bad weather, just soft people."
>
> Bill Bowerman

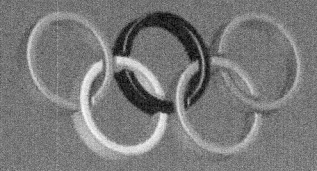

"I remember the last season I played. I went home after a ballgame one day, lay down on my bed, and tears came to my eyes. How can you explain that? It's like crying for your mother after she's gone. You cry because you love her. I cried, I guess, because I loved baseball, and I knew I had to leave it." -Willie Mays, 1 time Olympic medalist - track and field

"Winning is great, but being able to finish my last Olympic Games on American soil was very important. Even though I was injured, I didn't let my psyche get the best of me and cause me to doubt myself, so I was willing to pull every muscle in my body in '96 in order to get the job done and I came away with the bronze medal." -Jackie Joyner-Kersee, 6 time Olympic medalist - track and field

"At the two-thirds mark, I think of those who are still with me. Who might a break? Should I? Then I give it all I've got." -Ibrahim Hussein, 2 Olympic Games- track and field

"I give 'em the hip, then I take it away." -Jim Thorpe, 2 time Olympic medalist - track and field

"I got a bronze medal and I can't complain about that, the only African-American to get a medal in the Winter Olympics." -Debi Thomas, 1 time Olympic medalist - figure skating

"This ability to conquer oneself is no doubt the most precious of all things sports bestows."

Olga Korbut

"Every once in a while I run the Olympic downhill in Japan in my head. I think of how the energy is going to flow and then I make it all work for myself." -Picabo Street, 3 time Olympic medalist - skiing

ICE HOCKEY
1998 Olympic Games - Russia vs Czech Republic

"For so long I wanted to win the gold medal. Then I won. I had to figure out what was the new motivation to take myself to that place again." -Bryan Clay, 2 time Olympic medalist - track and field

> "Those who say that I will lose and am finished will have to run over my body to beat me."
>
> Said Aouita

> "You were born to be a player. You were meant to be here. This moment is yours."
>
> Herb Brooks

"I wouldn't allow myself to obsess over the physical pain or the heartbreak of missing the games; I wanted to focus on what I could, do-get ready to come back in 2010." -Noelle Pikus-Pace, 1 Olympic games - Skeleton Racer

"Some people say that I have an attitude- Maybe I do. But I think that you have to. You have to believe in yourself when no one else does- that makes you a winner right there." -Venus Williams, 4 time Olympic medalist - tennis

"Once you're in the game and it's a part of your life, you never want to leave it. But you have to be committed to be able to travel and do the things you need to do to be successful in whatever role you're doing." -Joe Sakic, 1 time Olympic medalist - ice hockey

"In a country where only men are encouraged, one must be one's own inspiration." -Tegla Loroupe, 1 Olympic games - track and field

"We all have dreams. But in order to make dreams come into reality, it takes an awful lot of determination, dedication, self-discipline, and effort." -Jesse Owens, 4 time Olympic medalist - track and field

"You have to have your wits about you and think quickly on your feet." -Michael East, 1 Olympic games - track and field

> "To give anything less than your best is to sacrifice the gift."
>
> Steve Prefontaine

"My salvation was a free gift. I didn't have to work for it and it's better than any gold medal that I've ever won." -Betty Cuthbert, 4 time Olympic medalist - track and field

CANOEING
2012 Olympic Games - Women's K-1 Canoe Slalom

"It is the inspiration of the Olympic Games that drives people not only to compete but to improve, and to bring lasting spiritual and moral benefits to the athlete and inspiration to those lucky enough to witness the athletic dedication." - Herb Elliott, 1 time Olympic medalist - track and field

> "Under pressure you can perform fifteen percent better or worse."
>
> Scott Hamilton

MEDAL CEREMONY

2010 Olympic Games - Women's Team Sprint Cross-country Skiing From left: Sweden (silver), Germany (gold), Russia (bronze)

"I've worked too hard and too long to let anything stand in the way of my goals. I will not let my teammates down and I will not let myself down." --Mia Hamm, 3 Time Olympic Medalist - soccer/football

"A trophy carries dust. Memories last forever." -Mary Lou Retton, 5 time Olympic medalist - gymnastics

Scott Frothingham

> "Victory is in having done your best. If you've done your best, you've won."
>
> Bill Bowerman

"Hills are speedwork in disguise."

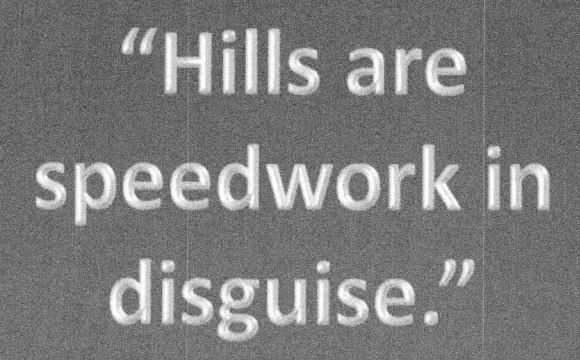

Frank Shorter

Scott Frothingham

"One shouldn't be afraid to lose; this is sport. One day you win; another day you lose. Of course, everyone wants to be the best. This is normal. This is what sport is about. This is why I love it." - Oksana Baiul, 1 time Olympic medalist - figure skating

"As a child I was very involved with sports and I knew at age 9 that I wanted to be an Olympic champion." -Marion Jones, 5 time Olympic medalist, track and field (later forfeited)

"They may become harder to achieve, but your dreams can't stop because you've hit a certain age or you've had a child." -Dara Torres, 12-time Olympic medalist - swimming

"At the Olympics, you there to do a job. I feel you should take it seriously. You should be respectful. You are putting on the red-white-and-blue and going out there to perform for your country." - Shannon Miller, 6 time Olympic medalist - gymnastics

"Getting started as a volunteer anywhere can be a challenge to a lot of people. The biggest hurdle is that people think they have to give all of their spare time. But if you only have a half hour, you can still make a difference. Assisting with small tasks is invaluable." -Jackie Joyner-Kersee, 6 time Olympic medalist - track and field

> "With so many people saying it couldn't be done, all it takes is an imagination."
>
> Michael Phelps

Scott Frothingham

"I succeed on my own personal motivation, dedication and commitment… My mindset is: If I'm not out there training, someone else is." -Lynn Jennings, 1 time Olympic medalist - track and field

OLYMPIC MEDALS
1988 Olympic Games

"Passion is a huge prerequisite to winning. It makes you willing to jump through hoops, go through all the ups and downs and everything in between to reach your goal." -Kerri Walsh, 3 time Olympic gold medalist - beach volleyball

> "You have to believe in yourself when no one else does - that makes you a winner right there."
>
> Venus Williams

"My brother was an elite special forces guy, so I think, 'If he can do it, I can too.'" -Georgia Gould, 1 time Olympic medalist - cycling

"The last mile was a cross between savoring the moment and just being really grateful that I was almost done." -Shalane Flanagan, 1 time Olympic medalist - track and field

"If my dreams can happen to me, your dreams can happen to you. Champions are not made on the track or field; champions are made by the things you accomplish and the way you use your abilities in everyday life situations." -Bob Beamon, 1 time Olympic medalist - track and field

CLOSING CEREMONY
1980 Olympics Games - The athletes entering the stadium

RECOMMENDATION

Don't Miss *Olympic Gold #2*
New! Over 140 quotes not in *Olympic Gold.*

Available on Amazon.com and from other retailers

ABOUT THE AUTHOR

Scott Frothingham is an entrepreneur, consultant, speaker, business coach and author best known for his FastForward Income™ products including *The 15-minute Sales Workout*™. He helps entrepreneurs, managers and sales/marketing executives position themselves for success through skills training and personal development -- along with providing tools for effectively and efficiently training and motivating their teams.

Some of Scott's other books authored by include "Olympic Spirit", "Success-ercize" and the 6 book "Words and Wisdom" series featuring great Americans such as Abraham Lincoln, Ben Franklin, Teddy Roosevelt and Mark Twain.

Scott Frothingham

www.ScottFrothingham.com

Facebook: **www.Facebook.com/FastForwardIncome**

Twitter: **@ScottFroth**

A Request

Can I Ask a Favor?

Thank you so much for reading my book. I hope you really liked it.

As you probably know, many people look at the reviews on Amazon before they decide to purchase a book.

If you liked the book, **could you please take a minute** to leave a review with your feedback?

Just go to Amazon.com, look up *Olympic Gold - Frothingham* go to the book's page and scroll down until you see the orange "Write a customer review button", click it and write a few words about why you like the book.

A couple of minutes is all I'm asking for, and it would mean the world to me.

Thank you so much,
Scott

Scott Frothingham

DON'T FORGET YOUR THANK YOU GIFT

To say, "Thanks" for buying this book, we'd like you to have

OLYMPIC SPIRIT

4 Inspirational Stories from the Olympic Games

R. Scott Frothingham

Go to this web address:
www.FastForwardPublishing.com/Thank-You-Olympic-Gold.html
to get your copy

Olympic Gold

FEATURED QUOTE DETAILS

"A champion is afraid of losing. Everyone else is afraid of winning." -Billie Jean King, head coach Olympic women's tennis

"Adversity, if you allow it to, will fortify you and make you the best you can be." -Kerri Walsh, 3 time Olympic gold medalist - beach volleyball

"Ask yourself: 'Can I give more?'. The answer is usually: 'Yes'." -Paul Tergat, 2 time Olympic medalist - track and field

"Don't put a limit on anything. The more you dream, the further you get." -Michael Phelps, 22 time Olympic medalist - swimming

"Each of us has a fire in our hearts for something. It's our goal in life to find it and keep it lit." Mary Lou Retton, 5 time Olympic medalist - gymnastics

"He who is not courageous enough to take risks will accomplish nothing in life." -Muhammad Ali,1 time Olympic medalist - boxing

"I didn't set out to beat the world; I just set out to do my absolute best." -Al Oerter, 4 time Olympic medalist - track and field

"I am building a fire, and every day I train, I add more fuel. At just the right moment, I light the match." -Mia Hamm, 3 Time Olympic Medalist - soccer/football

"I made a mistake but I came back to show the world that I'm still the best." -Usain Bolt, 6 time Olympic medalist - track and field

"I set my sights on making an Olympic team, not realizing how tough it was going to be." -Jackie Joyner-Kersee, 6 time Olympic medalist - track and field

Scott Frothingham

"I think the way to become the best is to just have fun." -Shaun White, 2 time Olympic medalist - snowboarding

"If you think you're done, you always have at least 40 percent more." -Lauren Crandall, 1 Olympic games - field hockey

"You never know what can happen. I feel like I have a pretty good chance, but you never know." -Carly Patterson, 3 time Olympic medalist - gymnastics

"If you win through bad sportsmanship, that's no real victory." -Babe Didrikson Zaharias, 3 time Olympic medalist - track and field

"Ingenuity plus courage plus work equals miracles." -Bob Richards, 3 time Olympic medalist - track and field

"It is better to look ahead and prepare than to look back and regret." -Jackie Joyner-Kersee, 6 time Olympic medalist - track and field

"It's always an honor to be able to represent your country at the highest level." -Basheer Abdullah, head coach Olympic men's boxing

"It's all about the journey, not the outcome." - Carl Lewis

"You have to expect things of yourself before you can do them." -Michael Jordan, 2 time Olympic medalist - basketball

"Run so hard you come in with bloody feet and missing toenails." -Rob De Castella, 1 Olympic Games - track and field

"Body does what mind prefers." -Lenny Krayzelburg, 4 time Olympic medalist - swimming

"Steady, ready, poised, winning." -Arielle Martin, 1 Olympic Games - cycling

"Success for an athlete follows many years of hard and dedication." -Michael Diamond, 6 time Olympic medalist - shooting

"It's not the destination, it's the journey." -Missy Franklin, 5 time Olympic medalist - swimming

"Surpassing my achievements feels incredible; I want to replicate that again and again." -Katherine Reutter, 6 time Olympic medalist - speed skating

"The difference between the impossible and the possible lies in a person's determination." -Tommy Lasorda, Olympic men's baseball manager

"The first thing is to love your sport. Never do it to please someone else. It has to be yours." -Peggy Fleming, 1 time Olympic medalist - figure skating

"You have to train your mind like you train your body." -Bruce Jenner, 1 time Olympic medalist - track and field

"You have to have your wits about you and think quickly on your feet." - Michael East, Michael East, 1 time Olympic medalist - track and field

"There's no such thing as bad weather, just soft people." -Bill Bowerman, trainer of Olympic athletes

"This ability to conquer oneself is no doubt the most precious of all things sports bestows." - Olga Korbut, 1 time Olympic medalist - gymnastics

"Those who say that I will lose and am finished will have to run over my body to beat me." -Said Aouita, 2 time Olympic medalist - track and field

"You were born to be a player. You were meant to be here. This moment is yours." -Herb Brooks head coach Olympic men's ice hockey

"To give anything less than your best is to sacrifice the gift." -Steve Prefontaine, 1 Olympic Games - track and field

"Under pressure you can perform fifteen percent better or worse."
-Scott Hamilton, 1 time Olympic medalist - figure skating

"Victory is in having done your best. If you've done your best, you've won." -Bill Bowerman, head coach Olympic track and field

"With so many people saying it couldn't be done, all it takes is an imagination." -Michael Phelps, 22 time Olympic medalist - swimming

"You have to believe in yourself when no one else does - that makes you a winner right there." -Venus Williams, 4 time Olympic medalist - tennis

This book was edited in January 2014 and the medal counts were sourced from Wikipedia.com. As such, the record counts for the active Olympians could be out of date if you are reading anytime after the 2012 Summer Games.

Olympic Gold

Photo Credits

COVER: London 128 British museum (28) olympic 2012 medals DAVID HOLT **David Holt London** October 11, 2011 Bloomsbury, London, England, GB Fujifilm FinePix T200 **Licensed under the** Creative Commons Attribution-Share Alike 2.0 Generic **license**

p. 8: The Olympic flag flying outside the Department to mark the start of the build-up to the Games. Department for Communities... July 20, 2012 Licensed under the Creative Commons Attribution-Share Alike 2.0 Generic license

p. 11:Olympic Opening Ceremony celebrates 'One World, One Dream' www.armymwr.com - Tim Hipps Licensed under the Creative Commons Attribution-Share Alike 2.0 Generic license

p. 15: Olympic torch carried by Nicola Bosio and Amanda Carreras in Ealing on 24 July 2012. Source GIBRALTAR'S OWN OLYMPIC TORCH Author jonathan manasco licensed under the Creative Commons Attribution-Share Alike 2.0 Generic license

p. 19: Basketball. Kris Krug August 10, 2008 Beijing, Beijing, CN Canon EOS 5D Licensed under the Creative Commons Attribution-Share Alike 2.0 Generic license

p. 23: 2008 Olympic Games equestrian in Sha Tin 21 August 2008 SourceOwn work Author WiNG licensed under the Creative Commons Attribution 3.0 Unported license

p. 27: Dive - Trampoline gymnastics at the Beijing Olympics. by cmaccubbin on Flickr licensed under the Creative Commons Attribution-Share Alike 2.0 Generic license

p. 31: Dawn Burrell lands in the sandpit during the Women's Long Jump competition at the 2000 Olympic games in Sydney, Australia, on September 27th, 2000 Sourcehttp://www.defenseimagery.mil; Details for 000927-F-8217W-005 Author Robert Whitehead, U.S. Air Force, Public Domain

p. 36: Headley Heath, on the Box Hill circuit. With a break several minutes 'up the road', Team GB riders are seen on the front of the chasing Peloton, with Bradley Wiggins the fourth in line.Peter Trimming Peter G Trimming July 28, 2012 Headley, England, GB Sony SLT-A77V licensed under the Creative Commons Attribution-Share Alike 2.0 Generic license

p. 38: Abeer Abdelrahman Khalil Mahmoud, Egyptian weightlifter, London 2012 Olympics. 3 August 2012, 15:36:09 Source Flickr: Olympics 2012: Women's 75kg Weightlifting Author Simon Q licensed under the Creative Commons Attribution-Share Alike 2.0 Generic license

p. 42: A happy home crowd cheers on their Canadian hockey heroes, who seem to be struggling to match the effort and intensity of their Swiss counterparts. s.yume February 18, 2010 Gastown, Vancouver, BC, CA Canon EOS 5D Mark II licensed under the Creative Commons Attribution-Share Alike 2.0 Generic license

p. 45: Men's Downhill at the 2010 Winter Olympics: Silver medalist Aksel Lund Svindal of Norway on his run. 15 February 2010, 12:08 Source Aksel Lund Svindal Uploaded by Miaow Miaow Author Kevin Pedraja from Seattle, USA Licensed under the Creative Commons Attribution-Share Alike 2.0 Generic license

p. 50: Pole vault olympian attempting the event Atos Atos International August 6, 2012 Nikon D800 Licensed under the Creative Commons Attribution-Share Alike 2.0 Generic license

p. 57: Curling Heather Harvey smilygrl February 18, 2010 South Cambie, Vancouver, BC, CA Olympus FE240/X795 Licensed under the Creative Commons Attribution-Share Alike 2.0 Generic license

p. 62: Single lane male swimmer in butterfly event at the Aquatics Centre Atos Atos International August 6, 2012 Nikon D800 Licensed under the Creative Commons Attribution-Share Alike 2.0 Generic license

p. 66: Nagano 1998-Russia vs Czech Republic The mens ice hockey Gold Medal Game of the 1998 Winter Olympics in Nagano. 2006-10-20 (original upload date) SourceTransferred from en.wikipedia Author Original uploader was Canadaolympic989 at en.wikipedia Licensed under the terms of the GNU Free Documentation License, Version 1.2 or any later version published by the Free Software Foundation; with no Invariant Sections, no Front-Cover Texts, and no Back-Cover Texts

p. 71: Slalom canoeing 2012 Olympics W K1 AUS Jessica Fox Canoeing at the 2012 Summer Olympics – Women's slalom K-1 Jessica Fox (AUS) 2 August 2012, 13:50 Source Flickr Uploaded by Miaow Miaow Author David Merrett from Daventry, England Licensed under the Creative Commons Attribution-Share Alike 2.0 Generic license

p. 73: The medal ceremony for the women's team sprint at the 2010 Winter Olympics. Left to right: Sweden (silver), Germany (gold), Russia (bronze)

22 February 2010, 08:15:13 Source originally posted to Flickr as Victory Ceremony- Whister 2010 **Author** Veronika S **Licensed under the** Creative Commons Attribution-Share Alike 2.0 Generic **license**

p. 78: A set of medals from the 1988 Winter Olympics on permanent display
at the Pengrowth Saddledome in Calgary. 19 March 2009 Source Own work Author Resolute licensed under the Creative Commons Attribution-Share Alike 3.0 Unported license

p. 80: The Festive closing ceremony of the 22nd Olympic games. Moscow's Central Lenin Stadium 3 August 1980 Source RIA Novosti archive, image #488317, http://visualrian.ru/ru/site/gallery/#488317 35 mm slide / 35 мм слайд Author Sergey Guneev / Сергей Гунеев licensed under the Creative Commons Attribution-Share Alike 3.0 Unported license

www.FastForwardPublishing.com

Made in the USA
Coppell, TX
08 June 2021